aspire

aspire

inspirational passages for
today's modern woman

d.j. posner

Copyrighted Material

Aspire: Inspirational Passages for Today's Modern Woman

Copyright © 2021 by D.J. Posner. All Rights Reserved.

No part of this publication may be reproduced, stored in a retrieval system or transmitted, in any form or by any means—electronic, mechanical, photocopying, recording or otherwise—without prior written permission from the publisher, except for the inclusion of brief quotations in a review.

For information about this title or to order other books and/or electronic media, contact the publisher:

D.J. Posner
Sarasota, Florida 34242
www.djposner.com
posner.easton@gmail.com

ISBNs:
978-1-7369399-2-5 (hardcover)
978-1-7369399-0-1 (softcover)
978-1-7369399-1-8 (eBook)

Library of Congress Control Number: 2021909635

Cover and Interior design: 1106 Design

*This book is dedicated to the women
in my life who inspired these passages.*

*And to all those women whom I have not met yet,
who will inevitably teach me even
more about sisterhood.*

◆ ◆ ◆

Preface

• • •

*E*very woman wants and needs to feel vibrant in order to live a deep and meaningful life. By intentionally paying attention to the present moment, we can find happiness, joy, and meaning in our lives. Finding your way to mindfulness is more than just sitting still and simply breathing; mastering the practices and techniques for living in the moment takes some effort, and the result is always life changing.

We all have experienced personal challenges that have affected our physical and mental health. These struggles generally compound in our minds as we visit them over and over in each waking moment. To begin, simply start a practice of paying attention to your senses during certain times in the day. For example, when you sit to take in your morning or evening meal, do so in quiet. Pay attention to the sounds and smells of the nourishment in front of you. Savor them. Slow down, and allow this more moderate pace to connect you with your senses. Is the aroma of your food pleasing? Does the sound of the crunch invigorate your enjoyment of it? If so, you are living in the moment! Next, apply this connective practice to your exercise routine, even if it is

Aspire

simply stretching or taking a walk. Listen to your footsteps as you walk, or feel your muscles expanding and unfolding as you increase your stretch. These simple sensory practices of mindfulness will lead you to the need and desire to meditate and transmit the feeling deeper within you.

The following collection of verse is resultant from my living each day in a mindful state. I offer them in a natural flow of speech and structure. My hope is that its narrative will help you develop an active inner monologue that hopefully leads you to a place of peace, centering, and encouragement. Try to find a little of yourself in each of the verses, and then connect to the feeling it evokes. That is living in the moment!

~ d.j. posner

d.j. posner

On Fulfillment

♦ ♦ ♦

A wonderful meditation began, and my words spilled out.

I thought . . . *What would I like to say to you?*

I take risks every day by allowing my essential-self

To pour out onto public pages.

I do this to be balanced, my power emergent, efflorescent

Because I retain the courage to put it on display.

I am a spirit who has always been on the karmic path.

And in my natural space, I am in service to God.

And from this I grow. And from growth, I flourish.

I have high ideals for my writing.

Graced with this, I am a communicator of truth.

On Receiving Goodness

• • •

I love the way my Aunt receives goodness.

Like the *Duchess* she is, it amasses around her like driven snow.

Being blind, her need for a helping hand is a familiar note.

Receiving goodness is not always something easily accomplished

Like spadework, it is difficult sometimes to allow yourself a "break"

To welcome another's care and concern to your bosom.

Finding the place in your soul to disarm your resistance,

While another graces your being with surrogate quietude.

For to seek out a journey that is not only of one's self,

Is, in doing so, where one finds the simple secret of "Let It Be"

Aspire

On Choosing Companions
◆ ◆ ◆

A call from a friend awoke me from my reverie.

She sends a photo by way of introduction.

She is adopting.

An exotic silvery-grey Shar-Pei with a beautiful face.

She is naming her after me.

I thought of the act, her embrace of a mere photograph.

Which perpetuated the practice of kindness in her reaching for this soul,

A soul who will accompany her on the journey throughout the coming years.

Communing with an animal spirit is a true practice of love and healing.

The created moments of happiness and joy become,

By way of their benevolence, nourishment for the soul.

d.j. posner

In Celebration of Women

• • •

Today is a day set aside to celebrate Women on an international scale

I think of the strides we, as a gender, have attained.

Once we were given the power to decide what to do with our own money,

Once we gained a genuine equality in wages, in stature, in voice.

Once we reached the apex and held onto the pinnacle,

We vested our fortitude in a world becoming less hostile.

We, the authentic gender, have birthed the next generation

And suckled their minds with encouragement and graces.

We have opened the doors and let them soar, trailblazing a path to tomorrow.

We have changed the changing world, by nurturing the idea that fair play, fair treatment, and no favor can and will bring about true parity.

d.j. posner

We were meant to walk in accord with each other.

By listening to the hearts of our silent sisters

And exploring the silence of that humanity,

We will flock together in victory.

Aspire

On Destiny

• • •

Along your journey, there are certain people placed in your path.

Souls, meant to nourish, extending their hand to hold on steady.

Like a storybook, you write your own destiny, steer your own boat.

The spirits who stay with you as you walk through your passage

Are kindred spirits—teachers and learners.

Your need for them will be equal in energy to their happiness in knowing you.

There will be no resistance ever felt,

And your journey will be made more certain in walking beside them.

d.j. posner

Aspire

On Comfort

• • •

I saw a woman in a crosswalk today.

Her smile was radiant, her pride worn high in her step.

She was pushing a carriage and smiling.

Her body still showing signs of her recent maternity.

She walked with great enjoyment, her pleasure apparent.

I envied her the serenity she displayed

No care or concern for the baby-pooch tummy

No signs of fatigue or weariness.

My envy melted away as I embraced the feeling of comfort

My skin warming at the sight

And I offered up a quiet wish

That we all should be so comfortable in our *own* skin.

Aspire

d.j. posner

On Lost Time

⋅ ⋅ ⋅

Who Is Saving Daylight Saving Time?

A Simple Sunday. The sun wakes shining.

A Sweet Sunday. The birds are singing.

A Sage Sunday. No work in sight.

A Snoozy Sunday. And lots of rest afterwards.

A Sweetheart Sunday. You and me wherever.

A Sleepy Sunday. Lights out at the end of the day.

The human condition benefits from time off.

But I am still missing One Hour!

Aspire

d.j. posner

On Gaining Ground
∴

Are you feeling all right today?

Is your thrust toward feeling empowered responding?

Have you found your way to "agreeable" today?

It is most important that, as humans, we find

And cultivate a resting place, a dominion for thought and virtue

In order that our values propagate in a fertile field.

For when we give roots to those values

We mark a place on our journey by planting trees of positive thought.

And through these saplings, we advance our humanity forward.

Aspire

An Homage

I am certain that my journey is fruitful.

I have met and walked with souls who have provided,

Merely by their presence, nourishment for a lifetime.

I have traveled with souls for only a short jaunt

And yet have extracted the essentials from those teaching moments

And walked on enriched by those encounters.

But the sapient souls with whom my locks have grayed,

The ones who will lie beside me at my departure

Are the ones who have cast their constant loving and shining light

Which illuminated my walkway, but also

Shined brightly upon my face and being.

These souls are my *beshert*, and are divinely destined spirits

Intended just for me.

On Appreciation
• • •

Gratitude becomes me.

I find it is easy for me to find gratefulness,

When I think of my children,

When I think of my strides in life.

Even though there have been tears along the way.

What are the tears we shed anyway?

Some shed in unabashed joy and glee.

Some shed in loss of someone or something profound

Some shed in frustration when an understanding cannot be met.

And others shed in appreciation of all of one's bounty.

This last manifestation is the one that ensures completion to

The seeker who wants to know God's love,

An onus one must encounter before ascending.

Aspire

A Heart Condition
• • •

A quiet heart, a listening heart, is a reachable, safe harbor.

Within us all, there lies a unique desire to connect

When we think using only our minds, we miss the fundamental action

Of attaining a listening, "thinking" heart

The world needs a connection between the two elements.

Body and Soul. This is the similitude of the two essentials

A parlance to bring us to a better humanity and intimacy with God.

Deep secrets will awaken, and from that, deeper understanding will emerge.

The center of a listening heart, a quiet heart, is the place where God lives.

Aspire

On Unwavering Courage
• • •

Courage is something that is demonstrated,

Worn on a lapel like a broach of diamonds.

It's daring, a response to desire within one's heart,

Such bold spiritedness is both placement and plodding of one's footing

Along a path taken while charting a long journey.

I have known courageous women

Women who have broken the mold of the conventional

Raised the roof over the mundane and plowed ahead

In fortitude and resilience.

I am so attracted to strong, purposeful women

Adroit with powerful shoulders and mighty constitutions.

I want to be able to reach that same pinnacle and

Scale that peak so that I, too, will be considered

As one who lived a life chock-full of pluck and bravery!

d.j. posner

Aspire

On Moral Support
• • •

There are women I have known who have held me up

On the darkest days and the murkiest of nights.

And women who have provided warmth and strength

When mine was wavering and indecisive.

These spirits, who have come and gone throughout my life,

Have conquered, captured, apprehended the negative forces

And replaced them with uplifting, soaring songs.

I have heard the melody of these songs throughout my days

And am committed to always listening to their rhythmic chant

To guide me in my quest for perfection, and my need for Enlightenment.

d.j. posner

Aspire

On Saving

• • •

I lit the good candles last night and asked to be infused

With a new direction.

Like magic, my vision cleared and expanded to see beyond

That which was holding me.

I set a table with the finest dishes and silver and asked to be instilled with gratitude,

Beyond the appreciation that I had been mindful of.

And in the mystic aura of asking, I was rewarded with

A deeply satisfying peaceful soul, thankful for every crumb laid before me.

I made the bed with the silken sheets, the ones I had been saving

As saving no longer seemed a viable or worthy option.

I languished in their specialness and unleashed my thoughts of waiting

For a future time that may or may not come.

And in that wakeful moment, I began to realize that things we treasure in life

All have their season and purpose.

Aspire

Music
• • •

Music ~ Gives a soul to the Universe

Wings to the mind

Flight to imagination, and

Life to Everything!

~ Plato

Aspire

d.j. posner

Unearthing Love
• • •

I love the act . . .
Of falling in love
Of beholding the tallest tree in the forest in wonder
Of learning something new.

I love discovering new people to embrace
And falling in love with someone all over again.
I love exploring the mystery of living
And working hard, and then ending the day with prayer.

But most of all, I love tears of tenderness
And through that, finding humility in all I encounter.

Aspire

d.j. posner

Becoming Free From Worry
• • •

I will not spend time today worrying about tomorrow

Or in wanting to change yesterday, because it is gone.

Instead, I fill today with happiness and my desire for a flourishing spirit.

And in doing so, put forth wisdom and peace of mind

In changing the world one heart at a time.

Love is an overflowing of healing grace

Do not sit and wait for it.

Go at it with an unstoppable force.

Be Fierce.

Be Brave.

Aspire

On Hearts & Flowers

• • •

A special someone brought me flowers today.

"To color my world," she said.

Gleeful, I accepted them in the spirit they were intended

No one ever brings me flowers, I thought.

And when I do receive them, it is usually in asking for forgiveness

Of some slight or harsh words.

Yet, this gift, one meant only to provide me with a loving gesture

Was a delight, both to my heart and my aging spirit.

Thank you, Belle

Aspire

On Being Observant

• • •

I am a woman who breathes in deeply

And exhales purposefully.

With every breath I take in,

I am expelling its goodness back into the world.

This practice is beneficial to my soul, too.

I listen to the rhythm, its cadence bringing inner peace

Each measure patterned with syncopated movement

And through its practice, my soul is nourished

And finds its way to a state of mindfulness.

Aspire

d.j. posner

A Paragon of Virtue
...

Today is a fresh, new day,

Displaying a brilliant beginning

Chock-full of promise and happiness.

How can I unleash this feeling of goodness

Onto others who will benefit from its virtue?

I take a step, and then another, and before I know it

I am prancing and carrying a pocketful of mirth.

Contentment follows me, and as I end the day,
  my instinct tells me

My prayer has already been answered.

Aspire

d.j. posner

On Witnessing Grace
• • •

Today, I feel a new awakening on the horizon

After listening to the laments of humanity

And feeling the surge toward change

The change in my own heart's cadence

Envigorated and left me with a warm, dulcet radiance.

Yesterday, I watched a young man

As he helped an elderly man cross the street

I thought, *Something is really happening*

And through tears and chills I heard these words

Kindness, Integrity, Decency, Sincerity, Respect

And all at once, I felt the world had become a better, more refined place

All from witnessing one simple gesture.

Aspire

Search for the Good
• • •

Encounter each person with the highest regard

Listen intently for the goodness from within

Every being is equipped with a thread of decency

There is no exception.

You may have joined in conversation with someone not sincere

But did you place your ear upon his heart? Listen.

The thread of our innocent birth remains with us always.

Life's beaten, brutish ways have taken toll on many spirits

That is not disputed.

It is up to the listener to isolate the thread woven in infancy

And gently unravel it, laying it out swaddled in Regard.

There, magically before you, a kinder heart will appear.

d.j. posner

Aspire

d.j. posner

Mothers & Daughters
• • •

I heard your voice, your genuine concern

For a daughter far away from your wing.

Every child has a need for inclusion.

As daughters, we did, too.

We must remember our spirit at that age

We let our timorous hearts give way to our, sometimes, reckless souls.

We felt our way through and capitulated,

As we learned life's lessons the hard way.

We enjoyed the ride and came out strong and content

With our accomplishments.

I see that your child, who is wild and deeply inspired, is still wary,

And that the world she inherits is a tumultuous one

It's best we remember that it is hard to be a daredevil,

When uncertainty is knocking at your door.

Aspire

Rest

◆ ◆ ◆

The ability to rest comes down to the condition of your heart ♥

*~ **Dr. Saundra Dalton-Smith***

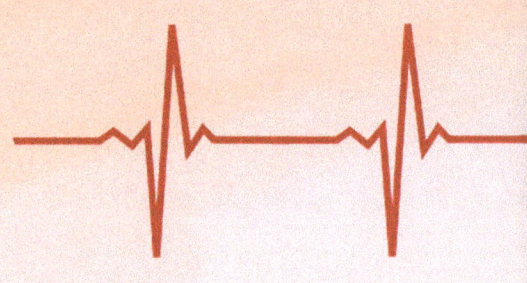

d.j. posner

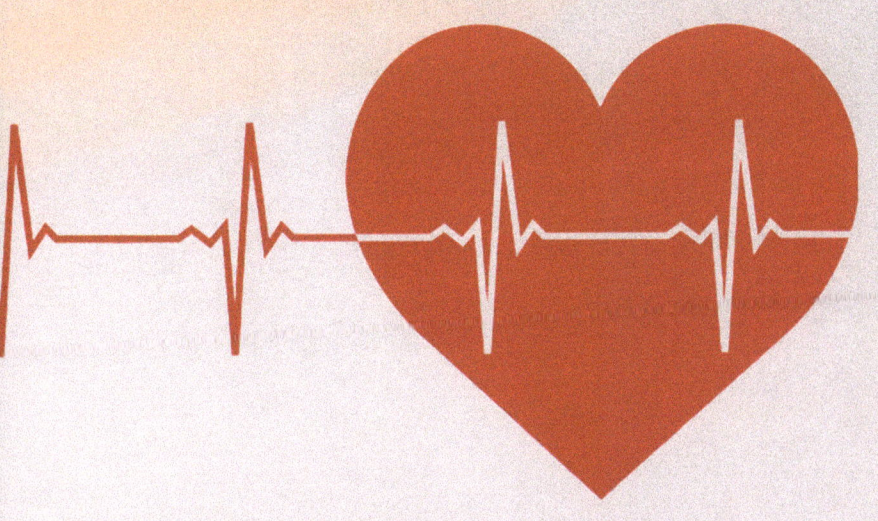

Aspire

On Solitude

• • •

I set the table with your flowers tonight

And it was as if you were with me. I miss you.

I'm not afraid to say that. I always lead with my heart.

I danced in the kitchen when I was waiting

Good food takes time. It, too, needs nurturing.

I envy you surrounded by all your lovies.

My quiet celebration, no less important,

Both will bring about renewal and the birth of fresh concepts.

But I still miss you and will welcome your return tomorrow.

d.j. posner

Aspire

d.j. posner

Lady Full of Grace
• • •

I have a friend who can bow her head and pray
Anytime she likes.
That's how comfortable she is in reaching God.
Her offerings are immediate and given
In each spiritual reflection throughout the day.
It is often, only in the morning or evening
When I bow my head for thanks or praise.
And as I examine this practice, it seems
I am limiting my access and relationship with God.

I admire her, this lady full of grace.
Her open door to the Divine.
I think we can all look to become more open
To let benevolence embrace us when the thought
Lights softly on our minds
Instead of waiting for the quiet of the day's beginning or end.

Aspire

On Practicing Stillness
• • •

Today I shall be still.
I shall wait and listen and be one with myself.
I will let the day unfold, and the coming hours ascend
On their own wing.
And in this practice, I shall rise high
Above all prejudice, above negative notions
Above politics, above coarse and crumbling persons.

Today I shall be still.

d.j. posner

Aspire

The Masks We Wear

• • •

Every woman is a warrior

Yet in reality we are geishas

And female dancers.

We show ourselves as sensual and empowered.

We are celebrated for our beauty,

But are we celebrated for our fortitude?

The masks we wear are fueled by our power

And we appear in all skin colors.

We are the jewels that give glitter to life

We withstand the blowing winds, and with that

We emerge with all we have to give.

d.j. posner

Aspire

On Seeking Consciousness

• • •

My broken, disobedient brain cannot help but improvise.

It is a normal course for me.

I struggle toward balance, toward steadfast and consistent equipoise

But never seem to achieve the exact pace of a resolute seeker.

I should be more forgiving, more tolerant of elusive obedience

For the creative workings of your heart begin with an improvised spirit

And from an embryonic spirit rises a fully evolved soul

Burgeoning, sprouting, and blooming with promise of the new springtide.

And so I honor and allow my disobedient brain

To guide my heart, so as to infuse my spirit, and by that,

Fulfill my quest for a nourished, sensitive, and conscious soul.

Aspire

d.j. posner

Leaving the Negative Behind
• • •

I have always been guided by my heart's desire

And in that, have followed those who seemed to believe in me

For some, I mistook allegiance for regard.

The miscue of my earnest and eager wagon,

Hitched to a star whose shine was not wholly mine,

Became the very hindrance of my spiritual growth.

Now that the years have passed by me

My understanding of those yearnings has changed

I no longer listen to the temptations, my heart's wants and wishes

But instead I listen to the stillness within its chambers

And am guided by the flow of its blood through to my spirit

And in that tranquil, quiescent moment, I find the meaning of Love.

Connecting with God
• • •

I listen intently for God's voice each day

And let my heart be guided by His gentle wisdom and encouragement,

His utterances, putting into words my feelings of self.

He has been my constant since the day I arrived and looked for His face.

The way His angels made merry, cavorting and reveling in my perfection.

And the lessons they taught me in times spent by their side.

I know now, and furthermore, given my poet's soul, have always known

Each day that is promised on this Earth is released to the universe.

So each day's importance lies within us.

If our days are invested with kindness and charity

And wrapped up in a spirit of giving without receiving,

Then we can build a bridge to an island of peaceful living.

And by the same token, if we covet and hold the gold for only ourselves

Its shine blinding our hearts from our duty

Then the days we release will mar the beautiful watercolor we are creating.

Aspire

d.j. posner

Sunrise/Sunset
• • •

The benediction found in the light of a setting sun

Is cleansing in its finality.

The day's conclusion promised as the sun takes its last bow,

Then closes the stage curtain and falls away into darkness.

The morning light burgeoning mere hours later is the curtain call.

Its waxing beauty amplifying the promise of another day

Is no less stirring to one's soul.

For in the artistry of the Creator

We are sanctioned to begin anew

Without the burden of yesterday's woe.

Aspire

On Lost Friendship
• • •

I think of you often, my friend, as I spill words upon a page
I remember you told me, "Don't run from it—embrace it!
Kiss it right on the lips!" I still chuckle at that.

I came to consciousness later in life.
My kindness and open heart arriving with the first strands of gray.
I envy those born with it, like you, my friend.

Having found each other along this winding journey
And having walked so many miles together, I wonder
How did we come to drift so many miles apart?

d.j. posner

Aspire

Like Mother, Like Daughter
• • •

In the bathroom last night,
I turned around and saw my mother!
I was so happy!
She had been gone for such a long time.
I sighed as I thought of all the times I had yearned for her.
And here she was, once again.

Like in a dream, she smiled at me, and then I understood.
In a fully awake moment, my reflection revealed
For when I saw my mother standing before me,
I was only looking in the mirror!

d.j. posner

Aspire

d.j. posner

Seek a Sweet Disposition
• • •

You are the captain of your time on this Earth
Choose well today and tomorrow, too.
Consider beginning your day with a spiritual practice
After the night has come to an end and the day is entering.
Center yourself, and listen intently to your own soul's song.

Look for people who bring out the best in you.
Let yourself be guided by the need for human connection.
Speak sweetly. And in those sweet words, develop kindness.

Aspire

d.j. posner

On Strengthening Grace

• • •

Arise each morning, and allow your faith to stand strong.

Straighten your backbone, and breathe in the artistry of a new day.

Beauty can be better appreciated while in the mode of goodness.

So find virtue, and arrange for it to be celebrated.

Whether alone or gathered together

Allow for singing, dancing, and exhibitions of gaiety; seek and allow for celebratory festivals

All this best describes the course for attaining grace.

And in finding the ideal human condition of rest, harmony, and accord.

Aspire

Letter to the Divine One

• • •

To my Creator

Thank you for the interesting work I will do today.

Thank you for the engaging souls I will meet as a matter of consequence.

Know that I am grateful for the love I find in today's hours

Thank you for the blessings you bestow upon me, as I bestow upon you a light to shine your glory.

d.j. posner

I am beholden to you for providing me with this
amazing life

For I am a seeker, and every day I step onto the stage
that you provide

I am carried by an indelible memory of good
and kindness.

I am grateful to you for awarding me new souls
to experience.

At day's end, I will lay my head down in mindful silence
as I seek the path to the dawning of the new day.

Aspire

On Acceptance
· · ·

There is a new kind of spirituality in the air

The need to follow it is imperative to my soul.

I trust in my writing and vow to never be led astray

Or allow others to threaten that vocation.

d.j. posner

As I have aged, I have become quieter and more peaceful,

And I have a more profound understanding of life and death.

Once reaching a certain pinnacle, the days until death finds us

Are nearer rather than distant.

The older I grow, the better I know My Divine, and the better I understand this path I walk.

Aspire

Jon Katz Words

• • •

I am a voracious reader, and it is sometimes in that act I come across a passage that speaks to me so profoundly that it compels me to act.

This is how I felt when I read my fellow writer's passage written in context about his dear, dying friend. I hope that you, too, my reader, will feel the same response and be inspired by Jon's deep-felt and reflective words.

Since the day I was born, death began its slow walk to meet me. It walks toward me every minute, without hurrying or ever turning around. People are so surprised to meet up with it, but they aren't paying attention; it is the surest thing that there is in the world.

~ Jon Katz, Bedlam Farm Journal

Aspire

d.j. posner

If I Could Do It Over Again . . .

I would do better

I would travel light.

I would spend more time in the presence of art and music

I would dedicate more hours to mental awakening

I would hold the beauty of the world with open hands

I would spend less time in isolation and more time in devotional prayer

I would spend more time in service to others

I would hold the Divine White Light and and emit its radiance to all I encounter.

Aspire

d.j. posner

On Heartache

• • •

Physical pain is nothing compared to the pain of
 a broken bond.

The binding straps of a promise, the ligaments meant to
 hold and cradle
Should not, in fact, be turned into a manacle that crushes
 one's spirit.
For it is with heartbreak that one must delve deeper
 to unearth
The threads, the strands, once woven to a life now hanging
 in the balance
A lone prayer offered to an empty sky.

That is the way of anguish, but allowing it to undergo
 examination
Leads to an understanding that there is no fight to the finish
There is only hope in closing the door softly
And walking toward a new beginning.

Aspire

Listen to the Music

• • •

Ask nothing. Just listen intently.

Become a receiver by being receptive.

Hearken as you tune into the voice

Of your creator,

Of your friend or acquaintance.

Be calm, be reposeful and serene.

By accepting another's thoughts,

Your voice, although mute, will be clearly heard

By all those in your presence.

d.j. posner

Aspire

d.j. posner

On Friendship

• • •

Friendship comes with its own set of ethics.

Standards that govern the conduct of both souls who dare enter it.

Beyond customary politeness, an orthodox behavior rises

To create the fabric for which parity will be cultivated.

In each encounter of a new relationship, I allow my surprise its space.

This, in turn, always grants permission to be grateful

And never to take for granted the delicate process of building

A framework for bonding my newfound friend to my soul

There is a fresh start in each new rapport I come upon.

By allowing space for the metamorphosis of my companion,

I pursue the act of reaching a harmonic accord

And in finding that ground, I proceed toward perfect affinity.

Aspire

On Grief
• • •

Grief, in itself, is a journey for the suffering souls left behind.

A grieving soul's spirit, once vital and wrapped in a blanket of hope,

Is now in search of comfort, the pursuit of which stretches far and wide.

Grief's most prevalent demand is in its need to be heard

Its mournful cries sounding out straight from
a wounded heart.

While it is said that . . .

*Better to have known love and lost than never to have
loved at all . . .*

Grief is the price of that love—the deeper the love, the
greater the grief.

This anguish is our reaction to a life that we believed
should never have had an expiration date.

And the guilt that accompanies this torment poisons
the well.

When a victim is permeated with this overwhelming burden

The consequence is scathing misery and deep sorrow

Haunting the memories of those whom we held so dear.

Aspire

On Guilt

• • •

Guilt is terrible poison.

An onus that holds a peculiar, vivid charm

While it wraps around a fault line as big as the San Andreas.

It is that anger, that useless emotion, which plies deep within one's psyche

And holds us to a past regret. It stays with you,

Harming the natural internal system of the body and mind.

Finding the path to recovery after a blow to our spirit

A blow caused by our act of harboring remorse and self-condemnation

Is a clear and absolving path. One must seek to exonerate and overlook

The vast crevasse below that holds the spurning river of contempt

And in this clemency one can discharge injury, and in that,

Restore quietude and serenity.

d.j. posner

Aspire

On Sisterhood

• • •

Sister, do you find my body soft and yielding?

I give my heart to you, and it melts and converts to sugar.

I become a peaceful, vital spirit whose center of emotion

Is raw and open. My outreach is selfless when I find you.

Your core, a rigid, unwavering goodness

Your wholesome nobility channeling your course

So that you do not wander too far from the familiar

The familiar that was to be your life's guarantee,
   your purpose, your intention.

This time, you will elect and choose with fervor

And stand where it suits you, planting your feet in rich soil.

I will stand tall among the forest, where the thicket
   of the wildwoods

Sport blossoms that you will recognize.

d.j. posner

Aspire

On Forgiveness
• • •

Another way to approach forgiveness is to begin each new day

Without concern for yesterday's heavy heart issues.

Begin each day by opening your eyes with the sun

As it lightens and slowly starts to warm the skin.

Encounter everything you meet as new, be an open heart.

Practice this art of not bringing yesterday into today.

Your steps will be lighter having left the melancholy behind

Meet the hours of each new day, of every new day, without judgment

And should you encounter yesterday's woes again,

Simply listen anew, and by that, find peace and, soon, resolution.

Works every time.

d.j. posner

Aspire

d.j. posner

On Struggle
∴

When struggle grabs ahold of you

When you become stifled and silent.

It is best to retreat to a place of safety in your mind.

Keep your thoughts in **Joy**,

Your spoken words in **Truth**,

And all of your actions in **Love**.

With that, the universe will be happy to oblige you

And will meet ALL of your needs.

It is the natural **Law of Attraction**.

Aspire

The Practice of Sacrifice

• • •

Would you give up the last French fry?

Would you place your last dollar in the hand of the needy?

Would you allow your ego to step aside to become a better version of yourself?

These things, these million little graces, generate devotion.

Whether spiritual or eternal piety

It is the sacrifice and the abstention that opens the soul to the Light.

Practice being devoted to this life's process

To surrendering and yielding yourself to service.

Find, in that routine, the magnificence of this world.

d.j. posner

Aspire

d.j. posner

On Absolution
•••

I believe there exists certain accidents of fortune

The forks in our life's path that predetermine for us

All that we can be.

It is important to always remember

To never harbor bad thoughts of anyone you have ever loved

Instead, allow for loving thoughts of those souls dear to you,

The ones found in your naked mind,

To be painted on your canvas in brightly hued colors

Next, pencil in those persons, places, and experiences held in disdain

And scatter them along the border of the frame of your masterpiece.

Thereby, you will not taint your work of art.

Aspire

On Moving Forward

• • •

I have lived in many beautiful places

All because I wasn't afraid of taking a chance on moving forward.

I love the life I am living. I always cling to its vision

When I am out seeking.

For I believe that when you truly know where you came from,

It makes it easier to get to where you are going.

And even though our path is divinely written

Albeit, tempered by free will,

It remains that each life remarkably affects another and so on

And so on

Therefore, your finest hour will always be when your soul has taken root

And is looking forward to the dawn.

d.j. posner

Aspire

Freedom From Religion

∴

It is a time of mental awakening, a time to make a pledge for tolerance

As humans, we are entering an era in which we need to apply the courageous tenacity of a comforting mother, and

Make ourselves a safe place from which to spring.

To begin this . . .

Let us cause a storm of change, and compose a survival guide for the next generation.

Prescribe a method of working together that will result in us remembering our common humanity.

And for those souls who live outside the confines of conventional religious faith, offer up an empyrean prayer so that cosmic enlightenment will be realized and shared by all.

For a spiritual life belongs to all of us, not just one faith or church

Aspire

d.j. posner

On Letting Go
• • •

My soul imprint is changing.

I am seeking quieter ways of being.

I am shedding those beings who bring my vibrations down.

I am willing to embrace new concepts

As well as unlearn old notions.

I will recharge from the clean elements around me.

I shall honor and fuel my energy for the highest and best good.

Everything I say and do will come from unconditional love.

Always reaching for unbounded love, redemption, and celebration.

Aspire

Following Your Path
• • •

Now, here I am after coming a long way on my journey
And although I am but a small being, my mind is strong.
Every day I am learning how to become filled with
Contentment, compassion, and appreciation.

I do this daily introspection in order that
One day I will become enlightened!

d.j. posner

Aspire

Human Responsibility
• • •

Each of us holds the responsibility for showing kindness to others and human care and concern for the world in which we live.

♥

Let us not allow our focus on material possessions and accumulating wealth be the cause of us failing in our quest for meeting this obligation.

♥

In accomplishing this, not only can our sons and daughters thrive in the future, but society in general can flourish.

♥

Each of us holds this responsibility.

Aspire

Making Each Moment Count
◆ ◆ ◆

Keep your thoughts on kindness, redemption and reverence.

It is a message that the angels who follow us recite clearly.

Hearing the angels speak this message is like

Bringing you to the comfort of your mother,

A sure and safe place.

This is what God has provided for us.

Think of this day as your last day. Make every moment count.

For to live victoriously is to manifest our greatness

And in doing that, we ascend upward one step at a time.

d.j. posner

Aspire

Solitude Is Not Selfish

• • •

Some solitude is essential to a spiritual life.

One must have solitude to become who they were meant to be.

Beginning anew is about leaving behind and changing course.

And any journey that opens your eyes and softens your heart

Is a journey worth taking!

Aspire

On One's Purpose
• • •

I write to keep my soul from loneliness.

I share my words publicly, and, in doing so, I am honoring my reader.

By allowing my reader into the sanctum of my heart's chambers,

I share the harmonious accord of Divine unity.

Girls like me adore the romance of verbs dancing on a page,

Painting a picture by a thousand words.

Truth be told, the art of *Linguistics* was likely my first love affair.

I have learned that these three things cannot be long hidden:

the Sun, the Moon, and the Truth

So I give you my transparency, and accept that all of us exist on this Earth with a purpose,

To fulfill and do everything that is meant to be done.

And allow our humanity to serve a Higher Being

d.j. posner

The Sun

The Moon

The Truth

Afterword

∴

This book was moved into pre-production during the pandemic year of COVID-19. In considering each verse, the thoughts of our feminine gender and the circumstances and course of events we have had to endure during the lockdown moved to the forefront in my mind.

The resilience I have witnessed, both in my own wide circle of sisters, as well as in essays gleaned from the media, have inspired me. The stories told are widespread and come from across the planet. We are all affected in one way or another.

The traditional role of women in our society was long defined as that of primary caretaker. And this held true in every country around the world. After all, women are the epitome of strength, love, sacrifice, and courage. However, the new age of thought which blossomed in the 1960s brought significant changes. Women became more self-sufficient, independent, and successful in their own right. Throughout the ensuing years, we, as a gender, have increased our awareness, sought higher education, and, as a result, now keep pace side by side with men in every walk of life.

Aspire

As we humans entered a new decade in a new millennium, the world suddenly vacillated. A killer virus invaded nearly every country in the world and brought with it vast changes. The roles we had known, the ones we had revolutionized, along with the strides we had made all took a deep backslide into a vast unknown. Sisters who had climbed their ladder, and from the pinnacle of that perch, were lambasted as the world slowed to a halt. No longer could we continue to make strides or suckle our children to grow their own strong roots. There were three meals a day to provide and no longer a paycheck from which to supply the ingredients. There were children to educate from the confines of the home's four walls. There were endless hours dealing with the anxiety and angst of our children and elders. And our carefully built lives buckled under the strain.

Fear and uncertainty were planted in every aspect of our female psyche. And yet we endured. We drew upon our strength and courage and applied even more sacrifice to ensure a favorable outcome. I, for one, looked to my

sisters for encouragement, and like magic, all the inspiration needed to finish this book was laid out before me like glistening diamonds.

My message to all the sisters reading this is to be stubborn in your commitments. Teaching can be a rough gig; think about it: it is an interminable job, one that never gets finished. Kids grow and change and need more education, which requires us to be as persistent as possible. Next, proclaim your presence with wonderful confidence; your shouts will be hard to ignore. Feed your minds, hearts, and souls—just like a blossoming flower needs to be pollinated, so does the female psyche.

Finally, from every impediment, hindrance, or ending, strive to create something new. Be a vehicle for wishes. View this cycle as an opportunity to reinvent and reimagine yourselves both personally and professionally. Allow yourselves to grow roots, bloom, and scatter seeds so new roots can grow. Hitch your wagon to a star! Shoot for the Moon! Simply put . . . Aspire.

About the Author

• • •

d.j. posner is a native of Washington, DC, and now permanently resides on Siesta Key, Florida. Known for her joy-filled positive and generous spirit, she shares with her readers her prescription for seeking and claiming that feeling for themselves.

www.ingramcontent.com/pod-product-compliance
Lightning Source LLC
Chambersburg PA
CBHW061146170426
43209CB00011B/1572